The Greatest in
BASEBALL

By MAC DAVIS

Cover design by Constance Ftera

SCHOLASTIC BOOK SERVICES

Published by Scholastic Book Services, a division of Scholastic Magazines, New York 36, N.Y.

Baseball's All-time Greats

Copyright © 1962 by Scholastic Magazines, Inc. All rights reserved. Published by Scholastic Book Services, a division of Scholastic Magazines, Inc.

2nd printing . . . . February 1967

Printed in the U.S.A.

OUTFIELDERS

CATCHERS

PITCHERS

At Bat with the Greatest

BASEBALL is America's national sport by popular acclaim. We watch it, play it, talk it — before, during, and after the season. For many, it has become a way of life.

Baseball begins early. Today more boys are out on the diamond than ever before. A recent national survey reveals that almost ten million youngsters between the ages of eight and 20 are playing regularly scheduled diamond contests, in organized competition. A handful of these boys will achieve the ultimate goal of all ballplayers — big-league fame and fortune.

Since baseball began more than a hundred years ago, countless millions have played the game. Of these, only a few thousand have reached the big leagues. Every state in the union has sent native sons to the majors.

Through the years the majors have featured many great players, but it's impossible to rank them in a way that would satisfy every fan. In fact, the quickest way to start an argument is to ask: "Who are the greatest in baseball history?" Few baseball buffs ever agree on the all-time, all-star lineup of baseball's greatest players.

You are about to meet 32 men who, in one sports writer's opinion, are the greatest heroes who ever played. Their unequaled achievements encompass the whole glorious history of America's favorite sport.

The highlights in the fabulous careers of these baseball greats are briefly and factually told. I have placed no false halos about their heads. Their glory as the greatest in baseball is of their own making.

How did these diamond immortals begin as ballplayers? What were the secrets of their greatness? What hardships, obstacles, and disappointments did they have to face and overcome before they became legends of the game?

For all boys who play baseball and aspire to big-league fame and fortune, I hope these authentic life stories will be an inspiration and a guide to the glory road. To all others who love the game and thrill to its heroes, these profiles offer close companionship with 32 of the greatest, most colorful, most fabulous, and most important performers baseball has ever had.

Perhaps not all of the players I have chosen will stand unchallenged as the greatest of all time. But for today, at least, they are as great as any others who ever played the game. From first base to third, from right field to left, from pitcher to catcher, these baseball greats have crowded the record books with their incredible achievements. Through their amazing diamond prowess they have helped to make the game of baseball what it is — America's national pastime.

MAC DAVIS

Original Hall-of-Fame members gather at Cooperstown, N.Y., June 12, 1939, to celebrate baseball's 100th anniversary. Back row (left to right): Honus Wagner, Grover Alexander, Tris Speaker, Napoleon Lajoie, George Sisler, Walter Johnson. Seated: Eddie Collins, Babe Ruth, Connie Mack, Cy Young.

Henry Louis (Lou) Gehrig

JUNE 19, 1903—JUNE 2, 1941

HE WAS "The Iron Horse" of baseball — the most durable player in major-league history.

Lou Gehrig began playing baseball as a kid on the sidewalks of New York. Her only son was Ma Gehrig's whole world, and she hoped that he would become an architect. To keep Lou in school, she took a job as a cook. But the powerful, athletic youngster loved baseball. Instead of houses, Lou Gehrig built a baseball legend.

While he was at Columbia University, starring in football and baseball, Lou's father become ill. Money was desperately needed for doctors and an emergency operation. Gehrig quit college and accepted a cash bonus of $1,500, thus becoming a professional baseball player for his home-town team, the New York Yankees.

When husky young Lou started as a big-league first baseman, he had tremendous power with a bat but was crude and clumsy in the field. He had perseverance and patience, however, and never stopped trying to improve his fielding. Through painstaking hard work, not only did he overcome his faults, but he became a flawless first baseman.

A player of model habits and great team spirit, he achieved feats unmatched by any other baseball star in history. On June 1, 1925, he broke into the Yankee lineup as a first baseman. From that day until April 30, 1939 — 14 years later — *he was never out of the Yankee lineup!* And when he quit, it was he himself who did the benching. It was the most incredible endurance feat baseball has ever seen. During that long playing period, Lou Gehrig was beaned three

7

times; had fingers broken ten times; suffered a fractured toe, torn leg muscles, wrenched shoulder and back, chipped elbow, and endured the pain of several attacks of lumbago. But never once did he use physical misfortune as an excuse to step down — not in 2,130 consecutive major-league games! This fantastic record of durability will probably stand for all time.

As first baseman, Larrupin' Lou performed other amazing feats. He became the first player of the 20th century to hit four consecutive home runs in a nine-inning game. Only Gehrig ever hit as many as 23 grand-slam homers!

For 12 straight seasons he hit over .300. In his lifetime he made 1,190 extra base hits, batted-in 1,991 runs, scored 1,888 runs, and walked 1,510 times. He also slugged 493 home runs, and wound up with a total of 2,721 hits, for a lifetime batting average of .340! He helped the Yankees win no less than seven pennants.

A quiet, modest player, Lou Gehrig never sought the headlines. Nevertheless, he became a national baseball idol and an inspiration to the youth of America.

Though The Iron Horse was one of the strongest men in baseball history, it was muscle weakness that struck him down at the height of his power and fame. Puzzled doctors called his mysterious affliction a rare form of chronic infantile paralysis. It robbed Lou Gehrig of his strength and co-ordination, and finished him as a big-league first baseman.

On July 4, 1939, aware that he was dying, Lou Gehrig made his final appearance on a major-league ball field. It was his farewell to baseball. Seventy-five thousand heavy-hearted fans and many civic and national dignitaries packed vast Yankee Stadium to pay him homage. With tears in his eyes, Lou stood humbly in the center of the field and thanked the hushed crowd for the many gifts which had been showered on him.

"They tell me I've been given a bad break by life. I've got a wonderful mother, a wife who loves me, and I've played baseball with the greatest teammates a ballplayer ever could hope for. I've had my share of good things. With all the good I've had, I consider myself the luckiest man on the face of this earth!"

Less than two years later, on June 2, 1941, Henry Louis Gehrig was dead, at the age of 38.

A nation grieved for this quiet hero of baseball. His locker in the Yankee clubhouse was turned into a shrine. No Yankee player ever again will wear Gehrig's famed number 4. Baseball's Hall of Fame immortalized him. Hollywood filmed a motion picture of his life accurately entitled, *The Pride of the Yankees*. And near Yankee Stadium, where for years this beloved athlete made imperishable history as a first baseman, there is now a quiet street named in his honor.

George Harold Sisler

MARCH 24, 1893—

FRESH out of college, where he had excelled in football and basketball, 21-year-old George Sisler came to the big leagues as a pitcher. In his first few games, the rookie southpaw won mound duels against some of the greatest hurlers then playing. He seemed destined for a great pitching career, but circumstances ruled otherwise. Sisler lasted only 12 games as a pitcher.

One afternoon in 1915 the manager of the St. Louis Browns said, "George, I know you can pitch, but the team needs a first baseman. From now on, you're it."

Sisler was reluctant to give up pitching, but he took his new assignment in stride. So well did he develop that he came to be regarded as the most graceful first baseman of all time. His smooth, classy fielding bordered on the fantastic. It was as a first baseman that George Sisler achieved Hall of Fame immortality.

A self-effacing player on and off the field, Sisler matched his astonishing fielding with phenomenal batting. In his first eight seasons as a major-league first baseman, he compiled an incredible batting average of .367! In 1920, he hit .407. Two seasons later, he zoomed to a lofty batting mark of .420!

Once he batted safely in 41 consecutive games. In 1920, he slashed 257 hits! No other player ever made as many safe hits in a single season! In the 16 years George Sisler was a major-league first baseman, he hit safely 2,812 times for a total of 3,864 bases. He also stole 375 bases, and wound up with a lifetime batting average of .340!

Called the smartest hitter who ever lived, he might have

become the greatest batter of all time if a cruel fate had not ruined his fabulous career right at its peak. At the age of 29 he was stricken with acute sinusitis, which affected his optic nerves and left him with double vision. He was out of baseball for a full year while doctors tried to save him from creeping blindness. He won his grim battle to see, but he was no longer the fantastic first baseman he had been.

Despite weak eyes, George Sisler was good enough to star in the big leagues for eight more years, still remarkable enough to bat over .340 — *twice.* In three of his last eight years he collected more than 200 hits; in his last season in the majors, he was still batting over .300!

Eye trouble cut short his own career, but he lived to see his sons follow in his footsteps. Dick and Dave Sisler both made the majors — one as a first baseman, the other as a pitcher.

11

James Emory Foxx

OCTOBER 22, 1907—

IN 1925, when the immortal Connie Mack was manager of the Philadelphia Athletics, he received a post card from his former third baseman, "Home Run" Baker. The old-timer wrote Mack that he was sending along a Maryland farm boy with the makings of a big-league player. When the 16-year-old youngster arrived at the Philadelphia ball park, Mack wasn't overjoyed. The boy wanted to be a catcher, and at that time Philadelphia already had two of the best catchers in the business.

But Manager Mack took another look when he saw the brawny farm boy hit a baseball. Young Jimmy Foxx could slug a ball a country mile.

Room had to be made on the team for a power hitter like that. Foxx was taken on — converted into a first baseman. Thus began the fabulous saga of one of the greatest right-handed home-run sluggers in history.

In 11 of his first 12 years in the majors, first baseman Foxx hit over .300. For 12 consecutive seasons, he hit 30 or more home runs. No batter ever looked more menacing at home plate than Jimmy Foxx. In spite of his fine personality and gentle disposition, Foxx was nicknamed "The Beast" because of his awesome strength. He could swing a big bat like a toothpick. Long home runs became a specialty of the Maryland Strong Boy.

Jimmy Foxx was so feared that pitchers would go to astonishing lengths to dodge his walloping bat. He was walked 1,458 times. In a game in 1938 he tied the all-time

THE SPORTING NEWS

walking record for a single contest: six times up, six bases on balls.

In 1932 he gave his greatest performance as home-run slugger. Although he was suffering from a painful wrist injury and could play only a few games in the final month of that season, he wound up with 58 homers! Only two players in history ever topped 58: Babe Ruth and Roger Maris.

In 20 seasons as a major-league first baseman, Foxx hit 534 homers! He also hit 125 triples, 458 doubles, and wound up with a total of 2,646 hits for a lifetime batting average of .325!

In three years he was honored with baseball's most coveted award: election as Most Valuable Player in his league.

James Emory Foxx's greatness as a home-run hitter and first baseman won for him a place in baseball's Hall of Fame.

Edward James (Big Ed) Delahanty

OCTOBER 31, 1867—JULY 2, 1903

THE SPORTING NEWS

THE DELAHANTY clan gave baseball the greatest "family act" in history. But of the five Delahanty brothers playing in the majors, the most famous was colorful Big Ed.

A spectacular and flawless fielder, the handsome 6-foot, 200-pound Irishman was also a fast man on his feet — he stole a total of 478 bases. No right-handed batter ever hit a baseball harder. His vicious line drives often knocked over rival infielders, and at times broke fingers and ankles. Big Ed racked up many unforgettable accomplishments with his big bat.

On July 13, 1896, he became the second man in history to hit four home runs in a nine-inning game. That memorable afternoon he hit for a total of 17 bases — a record that stood for the next 58 years. On two different occasions he had six hits in six times at bat. Twice he hit over .400, and five times over .370.

In 1899, while playing for the Philadelphia Phillies, he won the batting championship of the National League with a mark of .408! In 1902, while with the Washington Senators, he hit .376, to win the batting championship of the American League. What he did was unique: in all big-league history, Ed Delahanty was the only player who ever won a batting championship in both leagues!

In the old days of the dead ball, that magnificent first baseman hit 508 doubles and scored 1,596 runs. He wound up his 16 years in the majors with an amazing batting average of .346!

It was in 1903, while he was starring for the Washington Senators, that his fabulous big-league career came to an abrupt, shocking end. Ironically, it was his own doing.

High-powered first baseman that he was, Big Ed was also a high-living playboy who took his diamond fame and responsibilities lightly. His roughneck capers were the talk of the baseball world. During that last season he broke training so flagrantly that the Washington manager lost patience with him. To discipline the errant, the manager suspended him from the team for a few days.

Ed Delahanty went haywire over his chastisement. He deserted the club and boarded a train for home.

That night, aboard the speeding train, Big Ed created such a wild uproar that when the train made a brief stop at Fort Erie, Ontario, at the end of the International Bridge between Canada and the United States, the famous first baseman was put off.

In a weeping rage, Big Ed started to walk across the bridge. He was swallowed by the pitch-black night — never again to be seen alive!

On July 2, his mangled body was found pinned against a wharf some 20 miles from Niagara Falls. His strange and tragic end was never fully explained. Many believed he had fallen off the bridge and drowned in the waters of the Niagara. Others wondered if he had been the victim of foul play. Ed Delahanty's weird exit from the big leagues became, and still is, the greatest mystery in baseball history.

Adrian Constantine (Cap) Anson

APRIL 11, 1852—APRIL 14, 1922

FEW MEN ever played big-league ball as many years as Cap Anson. He was a star in the majors for 22 seasons. The first great first baseman in baseball history was the daddy of 'em all.

He was both an amazing fielder and a hitter. He won five batting championships, hitting .407, .399, .421, .344, and .342. He was the first player in history to make 3,000 hits. For his 22 years in the majors, he wound up with a lifetime batting average of .339.

Anson was also the greatest player-manager in history. The foremost strategist of his time, Cap Anson compiled an incredible record playing and managing the Chicago National League club: five pennants and four second-place finishes in 13 seasons.

The secret of his long life in the majors was rigid conditioning. No man in baseball ever had greater integrity, higher personal standards, or sense of dignity than handsome Cap Anson. He had a tremendous influence on the early growth of baseball.

A defender and example of the good life in an era when most players were tough guys, he inspired his players to give their best to baseball. But many were the times when powerful Cap Anson used his fists as well as his tongue to set down players who broke training. His players feared him, but they respected and loved him, too. He was one idol who never fell from grace.

In 1897, when he was 45, the amazing Cap played his

final season in the majors. So great was his popularity with the fans that $50,000 was raised by public subscription as a farewell gift for him.

In baseball's Hall of Fame, this "ancient" first baseman is enshrined as an immortal of the game. Moreover, Adrian Constantine Anson's contribution to baseball is still an important part of the national pastime, for it was Anson, back in 1886, who originated spring training.

Napoleon (Larry) Lajoie

SEPTEMBER 5, 1875–FEBRUARY 7, 1959

WHEN Napoleon Lajoie was still in his teens, he had already done a man's work. To support his widowed mother and her brood of seven children, he labored in a cotton mill and as a hack driver for a livery stable in Woonsocket, Rhode Island. But on Sundays, Larry Lajoie played sandlot baseball.

When the handsome French-Canadian youngster was offered $100 a month to play professional ball with the Fall River club of the old New England League, he gleefully exclaimed, "By Gar! From now on, I'm only going to play baseball!"

In 1896, before he was 21, Napoleon Lajoie was in the big leagues. He remained a star in the majors for 21 years. His diamond feats crowned him king of all second basemen. Above all, he achieved imperishable fame as baseball's most graceful player.

No second baseman has ever matched Lajoie's fielding. He moved around the infield with incredible grace; his big hands handled the ball with ease and assurance. He could make the most difficult play look easy. In 1908 he set an American League record for the most chances accepted by a second baseman in a single season — 988.

Although he was a 200-pound 6-footer, "Big Frenchy" had extraordinary speed. He stole 396 bases! And he was one of the most natural hitters of all time — a terrific right-handed batter.

In 1901, while starring for the Philadelphia Athletics, he became the first home-run champion of the American League, with 13 homers. That season he went to bat 543 times and made 229 hits, to win the batting championship with an incredible .422! It's still the all-time batting record for the American League.

Lajoie made his last hit as a major leaguer when he was past 41, in 1916. It was a tremendous triple. It was Lajoie's 3,251st base hit!

When he was 60 years old, the American League lured Larry out of retirement to star in an educational motion picture demonstrating proper batting form.

After 21 fabulous years of diamond glory, the king of all second basemen left the big leagues with but one regret: never once had he known the thrill of playing on a pennant-winning team.

In baseball's Hall of Fame in Cooperstown, only Napoleon Lajoie is singled out for his grace. The inscription on his plaque is unique: "Great hitter and most graceful and effective second-basemen of his era."

Jack Roosevelt (Jackie) Robinson

JANUARY 31, 1919—

BORN into the poverty of a sharecropper's cabin on a plantation in Georgia, Jackie Robinson first won fame as a sports hero while he was a student at the University of California at Los Angeles. He was a great all-round athlete — an All-American football and basketball player, a brilliant baseball and track star, and an outstanding boxer. He was to achieve his greatest fame, however, as a professional baseball player, for he became the hero of a "noble experiment."

In 1947, when Jackie first came to the big leagues to play second base for the former Brooklyn Dodgers, the eyes of the world were on him. He was baseball's strangest rookie. He was 28 years old, and he was a Negro. Never before had a Negro played in the majors. The fearless Jackie had been selected as the athlete to break down the color barrier in the big leagues.

No player in history ever had to show greater courage or had a better reason to make good in the majors than rookie Robinson. He was a target for every kind of bigot, humiliated and scorned at every turn. Even some of his own teammates refused to play with him. His life was threatened. But with exemplary conduct both on and off the field, with character, intelligence, dignity, and magnificent playing ability, the first Negro in major-league history forced a hostile baseball world to accept him as a star.

In his freshman season, Jackie played so brilliantly that he was honored as Rookie of the Year. Only two seasons later, he was acclaimed the Most Valuable Player of the National League. To achieve that coveted honor, he played in 156

games, setting a league record for second basemen. He topped all keystone men in double plays and led the league in stolen bases with 37. He made 203 hits, drove in 124 runs, scored 122, and won the batting championship with a .342 average.

Season by season, dynamic Jackie enriched his reputation as a great ballplayer. In 1951 he set a major league record for fewest errors by a second baseman. One of the baseball's fiercest competitors, he became the outstanding clutch player of his time. When the pressure was greatest, Jackie almost always came through with the key fielding play, hit, or stolen base. It was said he could beat the other team in more ways than any other man of his time. As a daring base stealer, he was in a class by himself. His spine-tingling feats on the base paths won many games for his team. He also became one of history's most versatile players, playing wherever his team needed him — at first, second, third, and in the outfield too. At all posts, he was a wizard with the glove.

So inspiring a player was Jackie, and so contagious was his eagerness to win, that in the ten seasons he starred for the Dodgers he sparked them to six pennants. In those years he slashed out 1,518 hits, bagged 137 homers, stole more than 200 bases, and compiled a .311 lifetime batting average.

When Jackie was past 38, though he could still command more than $50,000 a season playing in the big leagues, he decided he was too old for the game. He retired from baseball to embark on a successful business career.

Baseball made Jackie Robinson world-famous, one of the most celebrated heroes of his race. In return, he gave Americans a greater pride in their national pastime. Because of him, baseball was changed for the better. He had blazed a trail to the big leagues for all men to follow, regardless of race, color, or creed.

If he had made no other contribution, that would have been sufficient to earn him an honored place in baseball history. But in 1962 Jackie Robinson once again stepped into the limelight. He became the first Negro to be enshrined in baseball's Hall of Fame.

Rogers (Rajah) Hornsby

APRIL 27, 1896—

LATE in the baseball season of 1915, a 19-year-old boy from Texas reported to the St. Louis Cardinals. A second baseman, he had been bought from a bush-league club for $500. The rookie's hopes for big-league stardom looked anything but promising. Thin as a rail, Rogers Hornsby was almost 6 feet tall and weighed only 135 pounds. Although he was a fair infielder, he looked hopeless at bat. His stance at the plate was all wrong, and he couldn't hit a lick.

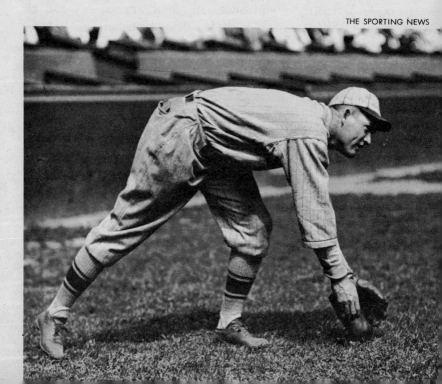

That skinny, weak-looking recruit had so much fire and spirit, however, and was so determined to make good, that the manager of the Cardinals decided to keep him on for a while. Rogers Hornsby remained in the big leagues for 23 years. He became one of the outstanding second basemen in history and the greatest right-handed hitter of all time!

For that serious-minded Texan there were no detours on the road to big-league fame and fortune. Baseball became his way of life. He lived, breathed, and slept baseball. Hornsby trained diligently year round, watching his diet carefully and sleeping at least ten hours a night. During baseball seasons, he didn't even go to the movies for fear of eyestrain. He never smoked or drank.

The Rajah was a sure-handed fielder with a strong, accurate throwing arm. He was a wizard on double plays, but his greatest glory was achieved with his mighty bat. As a hitter, Hornsby became tops of all right-handed sluggers. He had no weakness, he could hit to any field, against any and all pitchers. Some of his incredible batting feats have never been equaled.

He won the batting championship of the National League seven times. During one five-season span (1921-1925) he gave the most devastating hitting performance ever achieved by a major-league player. He won five batting championships in succession with marks of .397, .401, .384, .424 and .403. During that fantastic hitting spree, he went to bat 2,679 times and hit safely 1,078 times. He averaged 216 hits a season. His batting average for that five-year period was .402, a record that has never been equaled.

Hornsby's greatest batting feat was in 1924. He played in 143 games, made 227 hits, including 43 doubles, 14 triples, and 25 home runs. He finished that season with an awesome batting average of .424, the highest in modern major-league history!

He was the only player in the National League to bat .400

or better three times. In his 23 years in the majors, he slugged 302 home runs, made 2,930 hits, and wound up with a lifetime batting average of .358 — second highest in history.

With all his fabulous ability, Hornsby was a controversial player. He was outspoken and, in the opinion of many, lacking in diplomacy. Baseball was no popularity contest for the Rajah, not in either league or on any of the five clubs he joined. But regardless of feelings, he was so valuable a second baseman that once he was traded for more than $200,000.

With the power of his bat and his magnificent play at the keystone bag, Rogers Hornsby was an inspiring leader. He was a player-manager on four big-league teams. He piloted the St. Louis Cardinals to their first pennant and World Series championship. He also managed the Chicago Cubs to a flag.

When he was past 41, his zealousness and devotion to baseball were still so strong that he played and managed a minor-league club. Once he gave his players a brief, blunt lecture:

"Don't ever fool yourself about baseball. There's only one way to play the game, and that's by giving it all you've got, all the time. Only a sucker is satisfied to stay in the minors. The big leagues are the only place to play baseball. Get there as quickly as you can, and stay there as long as you can."

Rogers Hornsby knew, for he had 23 glorious years in the big leagues as a star second baseman. Historians will never dispute his right to an honored place in baseball's Hall of Fame.

Edward Trowbridge (Eddie) Collins

MAY 2, 1887—MARCH 25, 1951

THE SPORTING NEWS

HE was the only player who ever crashed the big leagues under a false name.

Late in the summer of 1906, when Edward Trowbridge Collins played in his first major-league game, he called himself Eddie Sullivan. He was still a college student, and he didn't want his mother to know that he had become a professional ballplayer.

After playing only six major-league games for the old Philadelphia Athletics, he returned to Columbia University to complete his senior year and receive his college diploma. Then, under his real name, 20-year-old Eddie Collins came back to play in the majors. He remained a brilliant star for the next 24 years, playing in 2,826 games. His many years of

26

active service in the big leagues is still a modern baseball record.

A nervous, jumpy player, Eddie stood only 5 feet,9 inches tall, and weighed a scant 150 pounds. He wasn't a flashy performer, but he made up in speed and judgment what he lacked in "color."

His fiery temper and fighting spirit made him an inspiration to his teammates. He sparked the Philadelphia Athletics to four pennants in five years, and the Chicago White Sox to two flags in three seasons.

When the stakes were highest and the pressure fiercest, Eddie Collins showed up best. No other player ever hit better than .400 in three different World Series classics. No one else ever stole as many as 14 bases in World Series competition.

Second-baseman Collins was one of the greatest base stealers of all time. In a single season he pilfered 81 bases. At times he achieved incredible feats on the base paths. On September 11, 1912, speedy Collins stole six bases in a nine-inning game. As if to prove that his amazing all-time record was no fluke, 11 days later he again stole six bases. During his fabulous career, he stole a total of 744 bases!

Eddie Collins also was one of the most skillful batters the game has ever seen. He could place hits to either field. A fine team man, he set the all-time American League record for sacrifice hits with a mark of 509. He was past 43 when he played his final game in the majors. He wound up with 3,313 hits and left a lifetime batting mark of .333.

Collins may have sneaked into the big leagues under a false name, but when he left, 25 years later, he was acclaimed one of the greatest of all second basemen. In 1939 he was elected to baseball's Hall of Fame.

Harold Joseph (Pie) Traynor

NOVEMBER 11, 1899–

WHEN Harold Traynor was only six years old and still playing with a rubber ball, he knew he wanted to be a famous baseball player when he grew up. As soon as he was old enough to play with the bigger boys in their sandlot baseball games, he earned the diamond nickname that was to become a legend in the big leagues.

Whenever his team won a game, the neighborhood priest treated the victorious ballplayers to pie. Since young Traynor was the star of every game, he always received an extra piece of pie. Thus he became known as Pie Traynor. That curious nickname was his trademark to the end of his baseball days.

Pie Traynor was barely 15 when he first tasted the joy of playing ball with real big leaguers. One day, while he was watching the Boston Red Sox in a practice session, the Red Sox third baseman left his position for a few minutes. Pie sneaked onto the field, took over at third base, and actually got into a few infield plays before the manager spotted him and chased him off the diamond.

Pie worked constantly to improve himself as a player. In 1920, before he was 21, his boyhood dream finally came true. He made the big leagues as a third baseman for the Pittsburgh Pirates.

Rangy, fleet-footed, sure-handed, Pie Traynor became the pride of the Pirates and the greatest third baseman in the majors. So he remained for 17 seasons.

No hot-corner man was ever smarter, fielded more brilliantly, hit harder, or ran the bases better than Pie. His fiery zest for baseball and never-say-die competitive spirit made him the grand master of all third basemen.

Traynor was also the perfect gentleman. Modest, soft-spoken, and polite, he never used profanity or lost his temper, no matter what the provocation.

His matchless playing sparked the Pittsburgh club to its first World Series championship. Pie was the first third baseman to play in as many as 1,941 major-league games. At his position, he set the all-time fielding mark with 2,288 putouts and 3,517 assists. He slashed out 2,416 hits and compiled a .320 lifetime batting average. He finished his fabulous years in the big leagues as the player-manager of the Pittsburgh Pirates.

THE SPORTING NEWS

Of all the great third basemen now immortalized in baseball's Hall of Fame, Pie Traynor is the undisputed monarch. To this day the name Pie Traynor is synonymous with third base.

John Franklin (Home Run) Baker

MARCH 13, 1886—

"HOME RUN" BAKER was a dirt farmer from Maryland before he came to the major leagues in 1908 to play third base for the old Philadelphia Athletics. A dour, bowlegged, 22-year-old rookie, he was so awkward and clumsy at third

that fans laughed at him. But ridicule did not discourage Baker. He was determined to make good as a big leaguer. He was an eager and daring fielder who wasn't afraid to roam far from his base to make a play. He wasn't afraid to stop hard-hit balls with chest or shins, nor was he ashamed to make an error. Although he moved like a crab, somehow he always seemed to be in front of every ball hit anywhere near him. He had fast hands, and he threw with speed and accuracy. Before long he became the most talked-about hot-corner man in the game. He was a star among the superlative stars in the Athletics' legendary "$100,000 infield" — perhaps the greatest infield combination known to the game.

The ungainly third baseman became a magnificent base runner. He usually stole about 40 bases a season. He achieved his greatest fame as a big-league hero, however, because of his home-run hitting. At a stage in history when a home run was a rarity, third baseman Baker made the circuit clout his own special artistic accomplishment.

In the 13 years he starred in the majors, Baker sparked his team to six pennants. He won his nickname — and everlasting fame as a home-run slugger — in the 1911 World Series, when he hit two home runs in two successive games. That dramatic feat of timely circuit clouting made third baseman Baker a baseball hero, not just to his teammates and fans, but for the ages. Thereafter he wasn't John Franklin, he was "Home Run" Baker.

But of all the great home-run hitters of history, Baker was the strangest, for he never hit more than 12 homers in any one season. In his 13 years in the big leagues, he hit only 93 in all. Here was a case of perfect timing; when he did hit them, they really counted. He became the only diamond great in the Hall of Fame to be identified solely as a home-run immortal. As long as big-league baseball is played, fans will remember Home Run Baker.

John Peter (Honus) Wagner

FEBRUARY 24, 1874—DECEMBER 6, 1955

AT THE AGE of 12 Honus Wagner was toiling in the coal mines of Pennsylvania. At 18 he was working as a barber. At 21 he was a professional ballplayer. By the time he was 43 he had become a baseball legend.

Honus Wagner was discovered while flinging rocks in a stone-throw contest with home-town cronies. The manager of a minor-league baseball club happened to see the powerful Dutchman scaling large stones over 300 feet. The manager was so impressed that he hired Wagner immediately, at $125 a month.

Honus was an obscure professional player for five years, until, at the turn of the century, the Pittsburgh Pirates bought him for $2,000. It was the beginning of a fabulous saga for a fantastic big-league hero.

Honus Wagner didn't look like a major-league player. He was ridiculously bowlegged, and had enormously long arms and huge hands hanging from a 71-inch, 200-pound body. Though he was one of the strongest men in baseball, he shied away from roughness and avoided arguments with rival players. He would rather be put out than spike or bowl over a player who got in his way. Playing in an era of tough, ruthless baseball, good-natured Honus Wagner played the game like a true sport.

"The Flying Dutchman" was such a natural player when he began in the big leagues that he could play almost anywhere with equal facility. Eventually he played every position except catcher, but finally settled down at shortstop — and became one of the best.

During his 21 years in the majors, Honus played in 2,785 games — more than anyone else in National League history. He made seemingly impossible plays. With his powerful throwing arm he often threw out runners while he was sitting or lying on the ground. He made 7,367 putouts and 6,628 assists. Roaming far and wide, he made only 799 errors in

21 big-league seasons, for an amazing lifetime fielding average of .946.

Bowlegged Honus Wagner, with his awkward stride, was one of the all-time greats on the base paths. He stole 720 bases. When it came to hitting he was a batter who had no weakness at the plate. For 17 consecutive seasons he hit over .300, setting National League records for hitting the most singles, doubles, and triples. He won the National League batting championship eight times — a league record that still stands. His National League record of 3,430 safe hits stood until 1962, when it was broken by another great: Stan Musial.

From first to last, Honus Wagner was a player in love only with baseball. At the height of his fame he was offered more than $1,000 a week to appear on the stage.

"I'm no actor and no freak. I'm just another baseball player," he said when he rejected the offer.

So great was his love for baseball that, when he came to the end of his playing days — at the ripe age of 43 — he remained in the game for 40 more years as a coach for the Pittsburgh Pirates.

Now he is a pillar in baseball's Hall of Fame. And now, too, in a little park just beyond Forbes Field in Pittsburgh, there stands an 18-foot bronze statue of the shortstop who became a legend in his own lifetime. The inscription reads:

"Erected in 1915 by the fans of America, in honor of a baseball immortal, a champion among champions whose record on and off the playing field of the national game will ever stand as a monument to his own greatness and as an example and inspiration to the youth of our country."

James Walter (Rabbit) Maranville

NOVEMBER 11, 1891–JANUARY 5, 1954

ONE OF THE smallest players in history, Walter Maranville became the second greatest shortstop baseball ever had. He topped all shortstops, however, for length of service in the big leagues, starring in them for 23 years.

Nicknamed "The Rabbit," Maranville was the most colorful, clowning player who ever donned a big-league uniform. On and off the baseball field, the 5-foot, 5-inch shortstop was a rollicking, fun-loving mischief-maker. Wherever he went he spread laughter, and he became the idol of the crowds.

Small as he was, Rabbit Maranville was an amazing fielder. He covered more ground than players twice his size. Playing the short field with a cocky nonchalance, he made the most impossible plays look easy. Spunky and aggressive, he feared no one. He defied baseball's biggest, roughest bullies. On the base

paths he blocked the most daring base stealers. Often the Rabbit would tag out a runner sliding into second, and then wind up triumphantly sitting on him.

This amazing dynamo was only in his second season in the majors when he sparked a floundering team to a baseball miracle. It happened in 1914, when he was shortstop for the last-place Boston Braves. A fierce competitor, the fighting Rabbit inspired his teammates to start a miraculous surge to glory. It didn't stop until the Boston team had won the pennant and the World Series championship. That season the Rabbit played in 156 games and accepted a record number of chances. He handled 1,046 balls, making 407 put-outs and 574 assists.

Sixteen years later, when the Rabbit was 38 years old, he was still peppery enough to lead the National League in fielding, with an average of .965.

When he was 40, he again led all big-league shortstops in fielding, and his superlative playing and fighting spirit sparked the St. Louis Cardinals to a pennant.

Countless and amazing were Rabbit Maranville's antics on a ball field. Just as startling and unbelievable were many of his wild capers off the diamond.

Often he appeared in public places with a pet parrot or monkey perched on his shoulder. He kept pigeons in hotel closets, put live fish in bathtubs, and allowed rabbits to scamper around his hotel. room. Once, just for a lark, he climbed out on the narrow ledge of his hotel window — 12 floors above the ground. Another time, on his way to the ball park, Rabbit swam across a river fully clothed, rather than ride across the bridge.

In 1925, when he became the player-manager of the Chicago Cubs, he was still the happy little diamond clown. He became the team's ring leader for every practical joke, every wild escapade. No wonder he lasted less than a season as a big-league pilot! But the clowning Rabbit went on puckishly, a grown man who was still a boy.

Rabbit Maranville was 43 when his big-league career came to a sudden and dramatic finish. He was playing a spring exhibition game when he tried to steal home with the winning run. The bulky young rival catcher blocked the plate on the play. Little Rabbit crashed into him and hit the ground with a broken leg. Though painfully injured, the fiery shortstop yelled to the umpire:

"I was safe! He never tagged me. I scored the run. Look where my foot is!"

Sure enough, his broken leg rested limply at the edge of home plate. When they carried him off the field, the game little guy said to his teammates:

"I had to stop sometime. Maybe this is the best way to go."

He never again played in the majors.

Perhaps the wild Rabbit wasted some of his magnificent skill as a shortstop by being a diamond clown. But no man ever had more fun playing in the big leagues than Walter Maranville. He lasted 23 years — longer than any other shortstop in history. And that amazing shrimp carved a man-sized niche for himself. In 1954 he was named to baseball's Hall of Fame.

Joseph Edward (Joe) Cronin

OCTOBER 12, 1906—

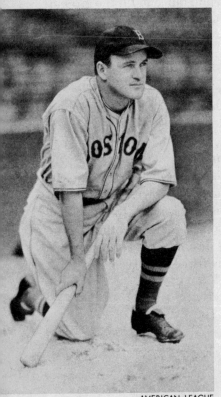

AMERICAN LEAGUE

BACK IN 1926, a poor gangling 19-year-old Irish boy from the San Francisco sandlots — Joe Cronin — crashed the major leagues with the Pittsburgh Pirates. Slow and clumsy, he was the worst-looking shortstop the Pirates ever had. Naturally he didn't last long in the majors. After only 38 games he was exiled to the minors.

However, square-jawed Joe Cronin was a stubborn lad, grimly determined to win fame and fortune as a big-league shortstop. He had tremendous zeal to learn and tireless energy for practice. He improved enough for a big-league scout to sign him up for the Washington Senators. At 22, Joe Cronin was back in the big leagues.

38

When Clark Griffith, owner of the Washington club, first saw rookie Cronin play, he was furious with the scout who'd spent the club's money for such a mediocre infielder and weak hitter. To divert the club owner's anger, the scout turned to Clark Griffith's pretty niece and said:

"I've been scouting for a husband for you, Mildred. Meet Joe Cronin."

Many a true word is spoken in jest. The shy rookie and the club owner's niece did indeed fall in love and were married.

Spurred by love and grim determination to succeed, Joe Cronin became one of the greatest fielding shortstops of all time, and — next to Honus Wagner — the hardest-hitting shortstop in history. What's more, he was such a good diamond strategist that when he was only 27 he became player-manager of the Washington Senators — one of the youngest big-league pilots in history. In 1933, his first season at the helm, shortstop Cronin managed his team to a pennant.

After seven great years starring for the Washington club, Joe Cronin became so valuable that Clark Griffith was persuaded to sell him to the Boston Red Sox for $250,000. It was the highest price ever paid for a baseball player!

For 11 more years Joe Cronin starred as a player-manager. In 1946 he piloted the Red Sox to a pennant.

Cronin is immortalized in baseball's Hall of Fame for his accomplishments as a shortstop. But further honors were in store for him. He was the first player from the big-league ranks to become president of the American League.

From the sandlots to the Hall of Fame, and on to the presidency of a major league, shortstop Joseph Edward Cronin created a success story in the American tradition.

George Herman (Babe) Ruth

FEBRUARY 6, 1895—AUGUST 16, 1948

THE CHILD of a broken home, George Herman Ruth grew up in the grinding poverty of the Baltimore slums. He spent his unhappy childhood running wild on the river-front streets — a tough kid who often got into trouble for fighting, begging, or stealing. Homeless and neglected, he was only seven when he was confined to St. Mary's Industrial School, a charity institution for delinquent boys.

There young Ruth learned how to play baseball. The game fascinated him. He became the school's star player. When he was 19 years old, he had become so skilled at pitching that a Brother from St. Mary's found him a job with a pro-fessional ball team at a salary of $600 a year. Under Mary-land law, the only way he could leave the school was to have a guardian assigned to him. His baseball manager agreed to be responsible for him, and from then on George Ruth became known to his teammates as "the Babe."

Only one year later Babe Ruth crashed the big leagues as a pitcher for the Boston Red Sox. He soon became one of the best pitchers in the majors. In his first three full seasons Babe won 64 games. So valuable was his pitching that in five years he helped the Red Sox win three pennants.

In 1916 Babe Ruth pitched and won the longest World Series contest ever played — a 14-inning game.

In the 1918 World Series he added to his growing fame as a great pitcher by winning two games and setting an amazing record for perfect World Series hurling. He pitched 29 consecutive scoreless innings. That performance remained unmatched until 1961.

WIDE WORLD

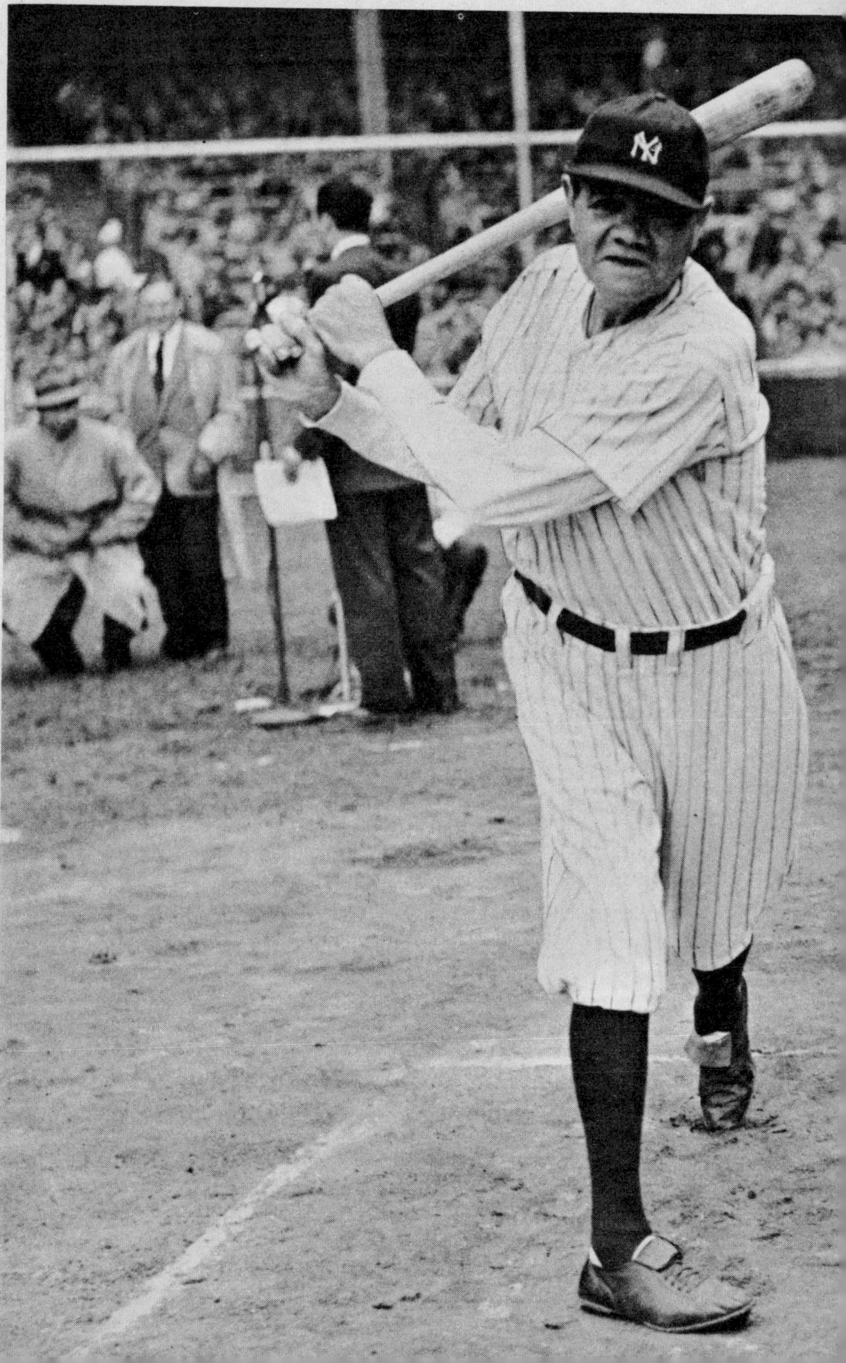

Although Babe Ruth would surely have become one of the greatest southpaw pitchers in history, he knocked himself off the mound with his tremendous hitting power! He began to hit baseballs so hard and so far that he was persuaded to give up pitching and become an outfielder, so he could play and hit every day. Babe Ruth became the most magnificent right fielder of all time.

His huge, 200-pound frame was perched on thin legs and small feet. He ran with mincing steps, but Babe was deceptively fast chasing fly balls. He was a sure-handed fielder, and his powerful throwing arm was deadly to all base runners. He was never guilty of an error in judgment, such as throwing to a wrong base. Quick and smart, he was also a crafty base runner.

In 1920 the Boston club, which only six years before had bought rookie Babe Ruth for $2,900, sold him to the New York Yankees for more than $125,000 in cash, plus a $350,000 loan. Thus began the fabulous reign of baseball's Sultan of Swat, and no real monarch in history was ever more revered than Babe Ruth. He became the greatest home-run slugger of all time.

For 15 years he held a nation in sway as he became the most colorful, most glamorous, most popular, and most famous baseball player the game had ever known. With his bludgeoning 42-ounce bat, he altered the character and structure of the national pastime. Millions of people flocked to the big-league ball parks to see Babe Ruth hit home runs. The Yankees built a huge multimillion dollar stadium for him to play in. This stadium became known as "The House That Ruth Built."

The rollicking and carefree Babe eventually drew a higher salary than the President of the United States. His name became known throughout the civilized world.

Once, before a game, he gorged himself with 18 hot dogs and a dozen bottles of soda. He was laid low with a stomachache that sent him to a hospital. Headlines in newspapers all over the world reported Babe Ruth's famous bellyache.

Babe loved baseball and baseball loved him, for he was the biggest and happiest "kid" in the game. And what incredible feats he performed!

He hit two or more homers in a game 72 times. This stands as the all-time record. He slugged 40 or more homers in a season 11 times — another record. Twelve times he either led or tied the league in home runs.

Babe was the first player in history to hit 50 home runs in one season. In 1920 he hit 54. The following reason he set a new all-time record by clouting 59 four-baggers. In 1927 he bettered this by hitting 60 homers, a record that stood for 34 years, and even then was broken in an extended season of 162 games. He frightened pitchers so much that he was walked more than any other player in history: 2,056 times.

The Babe was more than just the greatest power hitter the game has ever known. He also was a most consistent batsman. In the 22 seasons he played in the big leagues, he came to bat 8,399 times, made 2,873 hits, and compiled a lifetime batting average of .342! His thundering bat pounded out seven pennants for the Yankees.

The most beloved hero and the greatest drawing card in baseball history, Babe Ruth was most popular with the boys of America. They worshiped him as no other sports hero was ever worshiped. Wherever he appeared, kids mobbed him — to stare at him, to touch him, to beg for his autograph. He was devoted to all youngsters, and often went out of his way to see and encourage them. He was never too busy to visit boys in schools, institutions, and hospitals. He gave away hundreds of baseballs, bats, and gloves to starry-eyed youngsters.

On the eve of the 1926 World Series, Babe learned that a seriously ill boy in a hospital many miles away had expressed a wish to see him. Unannounced, Babe went to see the sick youngster. He stayed with him for a long time. As he left, the boy begged his hero to hit a home run for him in the World Series. Babe promised to do it. He kept his promise in the usual big way he always did everything. He hit four home runs in that classic. There must have been magic in that bat — the boy who was thought to be dying recovered from his illness and grew up to healthy manhood.

Babe Ruth was 40 when he finally called it quits as a big-league player. But he went out of the majors like the champion that he was. On May 25, 1935, the old and weary Babe staged an awesome farewell to glory. In three times at bat, he slugged three tremendous home runs out of the ball park. Within a week he left baseball forever.

He departed from the big leagues with an incredible all-time total of 714 home runs, 55 other records, and a million dollars.

On August 16, 1948, Babe Ruth's life was snuffed out by cancer. The whole world mourned him. But none grieved for him more than the boys of America. To them the Babe was still the greatest of all baseball heroes. He lay in state at the Yankee Stadium as thousands of weeping mourners filed past his bier, for a last look at the greatest home-run hitter of all time.

Of all the diamond greats enshrined in baseball's Hall of Fame, the most famous, always, will be George Herman Ruth. He stands immortal as a legend of America. As long as baseball players hit home runs, Babe Ruth will be remembered.

Tyrus Raymond (Ty) Cobb

DECEMBER 18, 1886–JULY 17, 1961

SINCE big-league baseball began back in 1876, thousands of men have played the game for fame and fortune. But Tyrus Raymond Cobb has been nominated by most experts as the best ballplayer who ever lived. Curiously, he became a player despite bitter parental opposition.

Born into a well-to-do and socially prominent southern family — his father was a state senator and a superintendent of schools in Georgia — Ty was expected to study for a career in medicine or law. But when he was only 17, rebellious Ty shocked his parents by becoming a professional baseball player.

"I'll be the best there ever was," the cocky youngster promised on leaving home. His unhappy parents hoped he would fail and return to his studies. Little did they know of their son's abilities.

A year later, In 1905, Ty Cobb came to the big leagues. The Detroit Tigers had bought him to be their center fielder for a paltry $500.

Driven by a strange, wild fury, Ty Cobb quickly fought his way to major-league stardom. Smarter, faster, and more aggressive than the rest, he became a big-league star unmatched in the history of baseball. Ironically, he also became the meanest, most conceited, most feared and hated player baseball has ever known.

Once in action, "The Georgia Peach" didn't have a friend in the world. A fearless brawler with a razor-edged temper, Ty engaged in numerous fist fights with rival players, umpires, heckling fans, and even his own teammates, most of whom wouldn't even speak to him. He was so irascible he couldn't get anyone to room with him.

Cobb aroused such violent hatred wherever he played that he often needed police protection. Once an assassin attacked him with a knife. Another time a mob of irate fans tried to lynch him. Ty Cobb fought and feuded the same way he always played baseball: to the hilt. In the 24 years he starred in the majors, he achieved feats beyond compare.

He was a keen student of the game, always a step ahead of his diamond foes. With scientific accuracy, he learned the weakness and strength of every opponent and planned his moves accordingly. A wizard in center field, nimble Ty was

so quick with his strong and accurate throwing arm that he often threw out runners at first base.

Cobb made a science of base running, too. No player ever used his legs the way Cobb did. With his flashing spikes, he spilled more blood and left behind more scars than any other competitor in history. At times, after a single or a walk he would score by stealing second, third, and home. Seven times he pilfered four bases in a single game — a record. For years he stole more than 70 bases per season. His career record of 892 stolen bases is not likely to be broken.

A picture athlete at the plate, Ty was also a magician with

DETROIT TIGERS

a bat. He played in more major-league games — 3,033 — than anyone, and no player in history ever made as many trips to the plate as Ty — 11,429. He set the all-time record for batting over .300: 23 consecutive seasons. Three times he hit over the magic .400, and 14 times he made five hits in a single game. Only Cobb ever hit 3,052 singles, scored 2,244 runs, and compiled a mark of 5,863 total bases.

Ty became the only player in history to win a major-league batting championship 12 times — nine of them in a row. He collected a record 4,000 hits. In fact, his fantastic total was 4,191 hits!

Ty remained the master batsman to the very last. At 42, in his final season with the majors, his manager gently suggested that old Ty Cobb, who was in a slump, step aside for a pinch hitter. Angrily, Ty snapped, "Nobody ever hits for Cobb!" He took his turn at bat, rapped out a winning hit, and continued to play for 95 games, finishing his last season with a .323 batting average.

During his stormy 24 years in the majors, Ty compiled an awesome lifetime batting average of .367 — the highest of all time!

He left the big leagues a millionaire and the holder of 90 baseball records. But away from baseball, Ty was restless and unhappy. As he mellowed with age, he tried to recast his public image of a diamond villain by using his wealth for good deeds. He built a hospital for his home town. He set up an endowment fund for the care of indigent patients. He chartered an educational foundation to give scholarships and financial aid to needy college students.

In time it may be forgotten that Tyrus Raymond Cobb was the most hated player who ever starred in big-league baseball. But history never will forget that he was the first player enshrined in baseball's Hall of Fame. He was what he had wanted to be — the greatest baseball player of all time.

Tristram (Spoke) Speaker

APRIL 4, 1888–DECEMBER 8, 1958

WHEN he was a boy growing up in the cow town of Hubbard City, Texas, Tristram Speaker gained local fame for his ability to ride horses, rope cattle, and shoot a rifle. But what he wanted most was to be a baseball player.

He was hardly 17 when he began to pitch for a baseball club in the North Texas League for $50 a month. Too soon, however, his good fortune turned to bitter disappointment. He was a failure, losing every game he pitched.

One afternoon after Speaker had lost still another game, this time by giving up 22 extra-base hits, the disgusted manager of the team barked at him:

"Kid, pack up, go home, and forget baseball. You'll never make it."

Discouraged, Tris gave up pitching. But he didn't give up baseball. He became an outfielder.

Two years later, in 1907, he was so good that the Boston Red Sox bought him for $400. He remained in the big leagues for 22 seasons and became the greatest defensive center fielder in the game.

Few ever patrolled the outfield more daringly, more efficiently, or with greater scientific judgment than fleet-footed Tris. He astonished the baseball world by playing center field so shallow that he was practically an extra infielder. In this position he robbed batters of sure hits driven behind second or short. Time and again the amazing Texan speared loping Texas leaguers and threw to nip surprised runners off second base. This was a feat unheard of for an outfielder.

When batters tried to cross him up by clouting the ball

THE SPORTING NEWS

over his head, they were usually disappointed. No center fielder ever went back as fast as Tris to catch long outfield flies. "The Gray Eagle" had almost superhuman instinct for knowing where the ball would be hit. His lifetime fielding average was .970.

The incredible Tris became more than the greatest defensive center fielder of all time. He also carved his niche in baseball history as a phenomenal hitter. He pounded out a record 793 doubles during his career. In 10,208 times at bat he slashed out 3,515 hits. Ty Cobb was the only other player in history whose hit total was higher. Tris also scored 1,881 runs and stole 433 bases. He finished with a lifetime batting average of .344.

Twice he sparked the Boston Red Sox to World Championships before he left the club to become the player-manager of the Cleveland Indians. The final day of the World Series in 1920 was the happiest day of his life. With his mother proudly watching from the stands, he piloted his team to the World Series championship and at the same time outplayed all the other stars of the game. As thousands cheered their baseball hero, Spoke fought his way to his mother's side and presented her with the winning baseball. It was the sweetest victory, and the most glorious moment of his fabulous big-league career.

Of all the diamond greats now in the Hall of Fame, none is more inspiring than Tristram Speaker. He began his baseball career as a miserable failure. But he refused to quit. With dogged determination he climbed the highest peaks of big-league glory.

Stanley Frank (Stan the Man) Musial

NOVEMBER 21, 1920—

STAN MUSIAL is the only player in history who actually cried himself into baseball.

His dream of big-league fame and fortune began in the drab steel-mill town of Donora, Pennsylvania. The eldest son of a poor Polish immigrant laborer, Stan was only 17 when he had to make the most important decision of his life. He had been offered a free college education on an athletic scholarship. But he had also been offered a contract to play professional baseball at $65 a month.

Papa Lukatz Musial violently objected to his son's leaving school to fritter his life away on a silly game for boys. But Stan stubbornly insisted that he had a future in organized baseball. When all his oratory and pleading failed to convince his father, he began to cry. He cried so bitterly that before long his father, too, was in tears.

Finally Stan's father relented and said: "For my son I wanted a better life than I have had. But if baseball means this much to you, I won't stand in your way. This is a free country, and you are free not to go to college."

For two years Stan Musial was a promising but insignificant southpaw hurler in the bush leagues. One afternoon, while fielding a ball, he fell and dislocated his left shoulder. It was his finish as a pitcher; his left arm was never strong again.

At 19, Stan was an unwanted, sore-armed pitcher with no job, no money, and no place to go. Moreover, he had a wife to support, for he had married his high school sweetheart. It was a crisis to test the heart and spirit of a full-grown man. But Stan was a determined youngster. He would not quit the game he loved. Ironically, he turned his tough break into a fabulous career. He became an outfielder.

ST. LOUIS CARDINALS

Late in the 1941 season, when Stan was 20, he came up to the big leagues to play outfield for the St. Louis Cardinals. From the start he performed like a player destined for baseball greatness. His hitting was sensational; his fielding spectacular; and his accurate throws mowed down base runners who dared challenge his lame pitching arm.

In his first three seasons as a major-league regular, Stan Musial sparked the St. Louis club to three pennants and two World Series championships.

At the end of only two seasons in the big leagues, Stan was already such an outstanding star that he was voted the Most Valuable Player of the National League. In his first six full seasons in the majors, Stan won the coveted MVP award three times.

As the seasons went by, modest and gentlemanly Stan Musial continued to grow in diamond greatness. He achieved astonishing feats.

In his first 17 years in the majors, he never batted less than .310. He became the first player in history to hit five home runs in a single day. Four times in one season he made five hits in a game. For 13 seasons his hits totaled more than 300 bases — another major-league record. He became the eighth player

53

in history to bag 3,000 safe hits. Seven times he won the National League batting championship.

He set the all-time National League record for durability by playing in 895 consecutive games. He became the only player in history to engage in more than 1,000 major-league contests at each of two posts: the outfield and first base.

Even-tempered and always a gentleman, he came to be known as "Stan the Man" and was one of the most popular stars in baseball history. He never made an enemy, and everybody wanted to be his friend. His magnificent diamond feats not only gave the nation a sports hero, but made him a millionaire.

In 1962, when he began his 20th season in the majors, Stan was 41 — the oldest player in the National League. He already owned an incredible array of records. For 19 consecutive seasons he had played in more than 100 games — a total of 2,767 big-league contests. He had gone to bat 10,202 times and had batted .300 for more consecutive years than anybody else in National League history. He had walked 1,500 times and scored 1,858 runs while batting in 1,811 runs. He had hit a League record of 697 doubles; in addition he also clouted 174 triples and 444 home runs — 1,315 extra-base hits. In all, he had made 3,401 hits for a total of 5,778 bases — another league record. (During the 1962 season he got his 3,431st hit, to eclipse Honus Wagner's 45-year record.)

Unquestionably, Stan Musial had earned the right to be called the National League's greatest player of all time. He ranked at the top — or very near it — of the all-time leaders in ten different important baseball departments. No other player in baseball history can boast of such a distinction.

Melvin Thomas (Mel) Ott

MARCH 2, 1909—NOVEMBER 21, 1958

THE SPORTING NEWS

MEL OTT was a baby-faced, 16-year-old country boy from Gretna, Louisiana, when he came to the New York Giants (now of San Francisco) to be a major-league catcher.

Though heavily built and barely 5 feet 9 inches, Mel was turned into an outfielder. Surprisingly, he became as great a right fielder as ever lived. He never played for any other team but the Giants, and he remained in right field for 22 years. He played that position with such all-around skill that he became famous in baseball history as "Mr. Right Field."

By the time young Mel was 19, he had already become one of the most feared sluggers in the game. The little Giant sported a batting average of .328 and a season's total of 42 home runs.

As he grew older, Mel revealed an awesome power with a bat. He performed heroics so often with late-inning, game-

55

winning homers that prudent pitchers frequently preferred to walk him. He was the only player who ever walked five times in each of three games. He was given 1,708 bases on balls.

The chunky little right fielder collected a bushel of records in his lifetime of ballplaying. He was the first modern player to score six runs in a nine-inning game. Mel achieved that feat twice. He played in 2,730 games, and made 2,876 hits, as he set league records for runs scored, bases on balls, runs batted in, and extra-base hits.

Mel also became the greatest home-run hitter in National League history. He set a National League record by hitting two home runs in a game 49 times.

He started the 1933 World Series by clouting a homer in his first time at bat, and he ended it with the winning home run in the last game's last inning. He was the only National League player to bag a lifetime total of 511 home runs.

Before Mel Ott left the big leagues he became the manager of the Giants, and remained their pilot for seven years.

In 1958, on a fog-shrouded road, he was fatally injured in an automobile accident. But the little Giant had lived long enough to see himself enrolled as an immortal in baseball's Hall of Fame.

In Mel's home town of Gretna, just outside New Orleans, there is a beautiful park dedicated in his honor. The Mel Ott Park helps keep green the memory of one of baseball's greatest heroes.

Joseph Paul (Joe) DiMaggio

NOVEMBER 25, 1914—

WHEN he was only 12 years old, Joe DiMaggio was already firmly set on a baseball career. His Italian immigrant father, a fisherman in San Francisco, wanted his eighth child to follow in his footsteps. But Joe hated fishing. The roll of a boat and the smell of fish made him ill.

He was 18 when his mother helped him realize part of his baseball dreams. She persuaded stern Papa DiMaggio to allow Joe to accept an offer to play professional ball with the San Francisco Seals of the Pacific Coast League. In his first season of professional baseball Joe was a sensation. He made minor-league history, in fact, by hitting safely in 61 consecutive games!

While Joe was still in the minors, a severe knee injury almost finished him as a ballplayer. Most baseball scouts shied away from him as a bad risk for the big leagues. But in 1936, when Joe was 21, the New York Yankees took a chance. They bought him for $25,000 and brought him to the majors to play center field.

From his rookie season to his last day in the big leagues, Joe DiMaggio was a spectacular star. He was the heart and soul of the fabulous Yankees. He became one of baseball's greatest picture hitters and a paragon of fielding ability. Baseball never had a more graceful center fielder than "The Yankee Clipper." With his smooth, casual style he speared fly balls for fantastic catches. And his rifle arm cut down a host of base runners.

Shy and laconic, he became a baseball hero for a whole nation. Gentlemanly Joe DiMaggio was the idol of millions

N.Y. YANKEES

of boys. Because of his heroic deeds on the ball field, he became the first player in history to be paid a salary of $100,000 a season.

Ironically, Joe was never lucky as a ballplayer. Dame Fortune treated him shabbily. Injuries and physical ailments dogged his footsteps. And at the peak of his brilliant big-league career, he left the majors for three years to serve with the Armed Forces in World War II.

Nevertheless, in the 13 seasons Joe played in the big leagues, he collected 2,214 hits, socked 361 homers, scored 1,390 runs, batted in 1,537 runs, won two batting championships, and wound up with a lifetime batting average of .325. Three times he was voted the Most Valuable Player in the American League.

The feat Joe achieved in 1941 was his greatest. During that season the Yankee Clipper went on the most incredible batting rampage in history. He hit safely in 56 consecutive games. It was the longest consecutive-game hitting streak in big-league history. It is an all-time record that should endure longer than any other mark in the annals of the game.

Joe's phenomenal hitting and unmatched fielding spurred the Yankees to ten pennants and eight World Series championships.

In 1951, when DiMaggio was 37 and still earning $100,000 a season, he retired from the game. He felt that he no longer could give his best as a ballplayer. No player ever departed from the big leagues more respected or beloved than proud Joe DiMaggio. He was more than one of the greatest center fielders in baseball history. He was the symbol of his generation — a living baseball legend, elected to the Hall of Fame in 1955.

Willie Howard Mays

MAY 6, 1931—

IN MAY of 1951, a few days after his 20th birthday, Willie Mays of the Minneapolis Millers was ordered to report to the big leagues to play center field for the New York Giants. Curiously, he was not anxious to play in the majors.

"You're making a mistake," he told the Giants' manager. "You don't want me. I'm not good enough."

On May 25, 1951, with only 116 ball games in organized baseball behind him, Willie Mays reluctantly appeared in his first big-league game. He had a miserable debut. In five times at bat he made no hits. What's more, he knocked over a teammate while running to catch an outfield fly. In his first 12 times at bat as a major-league player Willie failed to hit safely even once. He pleaded with his manager to send him back to the minors, where he had been a happy ballplayer. But the pilot told him, "Willie, we need you to win the pennant!" Finally he made his first hit. It was a home run.

Seven weeks before the end of the season the Giants were 13½ games out of first place—hopelessly out of the pennant race. But Willie continued to play with breath-taking excitement, as if every game were for the world championship. His blistering hitting, eye-popping fielding, and daring base running so inspired his teammates that before that pennant campaign was over, they'd won one of the most miraculous come-from-behind triumphs in baseball history. And Willie Mays became known as a miracle man of baseball.

In 1952 and 1953 Willie was out of the big leagues and in the United States Army. Without him, the Giants no longer led the baseball parade. But in 1954, when Willie returned from service, he again inspired his teammates. The Giants won another pennant, and then captured the World Series championship in four straight games.

In his first full season in the big leagues, Mays lashed out 195 hits, clouted 41 homers, drove in 110 runs, won the National League batting championship with a mark of .345, and wound up acclaimed the Most Valuable Player of the league.

Willie Mays of Fairfield, Alabama, was truly born to play baseball. Both his father

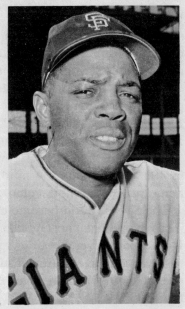

WIDE WORLD

and grandfather had been professional ballplayers. Willie was only 14 months old when he began playing with a baseball. He and his father would roll a ball across the floor of the family living room. Willie would cry when his father tired of the game.

At the age of three, Willie was given his first baseball glove, and he played catch with his father. At six he began to look like an outfielder. When he was 14 he was already playing semi-pro ball; and at 17, Willie was earning $300 a season, starring in the Negro National League.

The "Say-Hey Kid" — a nickname he picked up because he couldn't remember the names of the other players and used to yell, "Say, hey!" whenever he wanted somebody's attention — showed himself to be a most unusual diamond great. He didn't drink or smoke, and he was always in shape and ready to play. Always bubbling with laughter and happy

61

talk, and full of enthusiasm for the game, Willie became the most inspiring player in the majors. A famous rival manager once said of him: "Mays is the only ballplayer who can help a team just by riding on a bus with it!"

Season after season, Willie displayed his versatility and greatness. In 1955 he hit the most homers in the National League. In 1954, 1955, and 1957 he hit the most triples. From 1956 through 1959 he stole the most bases. In 1958 he scored the most runs. Once, he hit seven home runs in six games, and in 1961 he became the ninth player in history to hit four home runs in a single game.

The Say-Hey Kid became the first player in history to bag more than 30 homers and 30 stolen bases in the same season. He did both several seasons running. He became the all-time two-way threat of baseball history, and was the first player ever to both hit more than 200 home runs and steal more than 200 bases.

By the time Willie Mays celebrated his 30th birthday and completed a full decade in the big leagues, he had become a legend. When the amazing Say-Hey Kid began the 1962 season he had more diamond records to his credit than most great baseball veterans. He had hit more than 100 triples, collected more than 250 doubles, clouted more than 300 home runs, stolen more than 250 bases, and batted-in more than 1,000 runs.

On the baseball market, he was the only player ever priced at a cool million dollars. But even at that price he was not for sale. For as a center fielder, Willie Mays stands alone in his glory.

Theodore Samuel (Ted) Williams

AUGUST 30, 1918–

BORN in San Diego, California, Ted Williams didn't have a very happy childhood. He was the product of a broken home and had to struggle all the way. His mother, a bonneted Salvation Army worker who was known locally as "Salvation May," had dedicated him to the Salvation Army when he was still a baby. But Ted's boyhood dream was of becoming a famous big-league baseball player and the greatest hitter in history.

He was a gangling 17-year-old kid — 6-foot-4 and only 146 pounds — when he left high school to play professional baseball. A well-meaning baseball scout told his mother: "Mrs. Williams, if you let that boy of yours play pro ball, it will kill him!"

In 1939, when he was 20, Ted made his debut in the big leagues as a left fielder for the Boston Red Sox.

An outspoken youngster with an overwhelming sense of his own ability as a ballplayer, Ted Williams became one of baseball's most controversial players. Temperamental and highly sensitive, he irked the fans and feuded with baseball reporters. Many times he was fined for his surly petulance and angry outbursts. Once he was fined $5,000 for rude behavior — the highest fine of its kind in baseball history.

He wasted no time in becoming one of the most outstanding players in history, and as great a hitter as ever stepped to the plate in major-league competition. At the end of his first season in the big leagues Ted had a batting average of .327. He had hit 31 home runs, had led the American League in runs batted in, and had been acclaimed the Rookie of the

RED SOX

Year. They nicknamed him "The Splendid Splinter."

The following season Ted hit a lofty .344 to show the baseball world that he was destined to become one of its greatest hitters. And in his third season, he clearly revealed his greatness as a batsman. Left-fielder Williams came down to the final day of that 1941 season with a batting average standing at exactly .400! It was a phenomenal achievement for a 23-year-old. The Red Sox still had to play a double-header to complete the season, and Ted was advised to sit out the final two games to protect his batting mark. But to his everlasting credit, cocky Ted insisted on playing.

"I don't want anybody saying I made my .400 average while hiding in the dugout. I don't want to win a batting championship sitting on the bench. If I can't keep on hitting all through the season, then I don't deserve a batting title. I'll play!"

Play he did, and on that memorable day he went to bat eight times, lashed out six hits, and wound up a true champion with a batting average of .406 — to win his first major league batting title. Since then, there hasn't been another .400 hitter in the big leagues.

Ted's pell-mell rush to fame as one of baseball's greatest hitters continued unabated. The following season he not only won his second major-league batting championship, he wound up wearing the triple crown of the majors — first in batting, first in hitting home runs, and first in runs batted in.

After four of the most glorious seasons a player ever had, left-fielder Williams left the big leagues for bigger game. He joined the United States Marines as a fighter pilot in World War II. Three years were to pass before Ted returned to play in the majors. When he did get back to baseball, however, he reclaimed his fame as the greatest hitter in the game. He captured four more batting championships, won another triple crown of the majors, and was four times voted Most Valuable Player. He set an astonishing number of diamond records.

Pitchers paid tribute to his batting perfection; they lavished on him more than 100 bases on balls in 11 seasons. During his years as a big leaguer, Ted Williams drew more walks than any other player in history. He became the all-time on-base champion. Once he was walked in 19 consecutive games — an all-time record. Another time he got on base 16 straight times. No wonder he became the highest-paid ballplayer in history — $125,000 a season.

When Ted was 34 he again left the big leagues to serve his country as a fighter pilot. He flew 39 missions in the Korean War. Two years passed before he returned to the majors. Once more he performed batting wonders.

Ted was 39 when he captured his fifth batting championship. It was a unique feat. He was the oldest player in history to win a major-league batting title. The following season incredible Ted won his sixth batting championship!

On September 26, 1960, when left-fielder Ted Williams was 42 years old, he played his last major-league game. He went out of baseball in a blaze of glory. In his final time at bat he clouted one of the longest home runs ever hit. It was the 521st homer of his fabulous career. He finished with an astonishing lifetime batting average of .344.

"All I want out of life," said Ted when he first came to the big leagues, "is that when I walk down the street, folks will say — there goes the greatest hitter who ever lived!"

When he left the big leagues 21 years later, outfielder Williams had come mighty close to achieving his youthful ambition. "The Splendid Splinter" is one of the most admired heroes in baseball history. He's in the record books as one of the greatest of all hitters.

Mickey Charles Mantle

OCTOBER 20, 1931—

NO PLAYER in history had to overcome more mental torment or physical pain in his struggle for big-league greatness than did Mickey Mantle.

When Mickey was born in Spavinaw, Oklahoma, his father told everyone he would make his son a professional ballplayer. Mickey was only five years old when his ambitious father began teaching him how to swing a baseball bat, and hit both left- and right-handed. No boy ever tried harder to become a good ballplayer than Mickey — that was the way his Pa wanted it. The fear of failing in his father's eyes filled Mickey with terrors that plagued him throughout his youth. He was driven by a dream of baseball perfection.

While still in high school and playing in an amateur baseball league, Mickey was spotted by a scout for the New York Yankees. He was signed to a pro contract for a bonus of $1,300.

Mickey came to pro baseball afflicted with chronic osteomyelitis of the left leg — a bone-marrow inflammation that rarely left him free from pain. He never played in games without his leg heavily bandaged. Yet he never dogged it on a ball field. The muscular country boy had tremendous speed and awesome power with a bat.

Mickey was 19 when he came to the big leagues, in 1951, to play for the New York Yankees. From the beginning he was billed as a star. Everybody expected the rookie wonder to perform marvels. Although he had always been a shortstop, Mickey was suddenly forced to play center field. He had to

learn quickly how to be an outfielder. He did. He drove himself fiercely to live up to expectations.

In spite of the bad leg, a trick knee that could pop out on him any time, and the fear that any game might be his last as a big leaguer, hard-luck Mickey became one of the greatest center fielders in the majors.

In his first full season as a Yankee center fielder, he hit

over .300 and clouted 23 home runs. He was a speedboy on the bases and a ball hawk in the field. With every passing season, Mickey's fame as a center fielder grew.

He became the greatest and most powerful switch-hitter in baseball history. No switch hitter ever clouted as many home runs. Batting left- and right-handed during the same game, he belted homers for incredible distances. His harvest of switch-hitting four-baggers introduced the "tape-measure" home run to baseball. They had to be measured to be believed. In a game in 1953, Mickey socked a homer that traveled 565 feet from home plate. It was the longest home run ever hit. The ball was recovered and placed on exhibition in baseball's Hall of Fame at Cooperstown.

In 1956 he became the ninth player in history to capture the triple crown of the majors. He won the batting championship with a mark of .353, drove in the most runs (130), and clouted the most home runs (52). For good measure, he also scored 132 runs.

Again and again he led his league in slugging, and bases on balls. Twice he hit more than 50 home runs in a season. Twice he won the Most Valuable Player award. By the end of the 1961 season, Mickey had belted 374 home runs, and he had become a superstar earning $85,000 a year.

In his first 11 seasons in the big leagues, center-fielder Mantle sparked the Yankees to nine pennants and seven World Series championships.

No player ever achieved greater fame under more adverse conditions than stout-hearted Mickey. No switch-hitting slugger in history ever hit as many mighty home runs as this courageous center fielder.

Lawrence Peter (Yogi) Berra

MAY 12, 1925—

MIRACLES happen in big-league baseball. Take Yogi Berra for example.

The son of poor immigrant parents, Yogi grew up on the Hill, a tough Italian section in St. Louis. His boyhood dream was to become a professional baseball player. His father, a bricklayer, was scornful of such youthful ambition. He wanted Yogi to become a laborer so he could make good money.

When he was 17 and playing sandlot ball, Yogi was offered $90 a month to play for a New York Yankees' farm club. Despite his parents' protests, Yogi grabbed the golden opportunity for baseball fame and fortune. But it was no short and easy road to the big leagues.

For several years Yogi was lost in the obscurity of the minors. Finally, late in the 1946 season, the call came to report to the majors.

Knock-kneed, thick-shouldered, and homely, Yogi looked like a comic strip character when he first donned a big-league uniform. The little catcher became a ready butt for jokes. Rival players taunted him with cruel personal insults. Even his own teammates laughed at him. They poked fun at his ignorance, his dumb remarks, and his childlike gullibility. All agreed that Yogi was hardly a typical player for the fabulous Yankees, and that he would disgrace the noble tradition of the greatest pennant-winning club in history.

The awkward rookie catcher was a sad specimen. He misjudged fly balls, dropped easy pops, fell down chasing bunts, and threw wildly to the bases. Moreover, his stance at bat was peculiar, and he swung at bad balls. But the ugly-duckling catcher believed in himself, and was determined to make good in the big leagues.

Ignoring the abuse and ridicule, Yogi plugged on tirelessly. He had a zest for learning, an enthusiastic taste for his daily task, and a happy love of baseball. Few in the game had a better disposition. As the seasons went by, Yogi steadily improved. Eventually, he became recognized as one of the smartest and best-fielding catchers in baseball.

As he continued to grow in stature as a big-league catcher, Yogi also became baseball's pet player. Everybody discovered

N.Y. YANKEES

that the ugly little backstop was a wonderful person, with charm, character, and a sense of humor. He was a modest player without affectation or pretense. Fans everywhere admired him, and players from all teams grew fond of him. Even the umpires came to like and respect him. Yogi's funny remarks, odd mannerisms, and innocent verbal boners became treasured nuggets.

With the passing years, Yogi became more than a national baseball idol and the highest-paid catcher in big-league history. He became the greatest catcher of all time. He set records beyond the feats of all the great backstops in history.

No catcher ever played in as many consecutive major-league games without committing an error as did Yogi Berra.

71

He set an all-time mark of 148. He set the all-time record for most chances accepted by a big league backstop — 8,973. Time and time again he topped all receivers in double plays.

Yogi became the first catcher in history to make 2,000 hits. No backstop ever hit as many home runs as he did. In his first 15 seasons in the majors, he belted 340 four-baggers. He became the first catcher to win the Most Valuable Player Award three times.

By the end of the 1961 season Yogi had helped the Yankees win 12 pennants and nine World Series championships. He had also established himself as the king of the World Series, for he had become the greatest World Series performer of all time, holding more series records than any other player in history.

Only Yogi ever played in 12 post-season classics, and only he ever appeared in as many as 72 World Series games. He set an all-time record for most times at bat (256), most one-base hits (49), most doubles (10), most total hits (71), most runs (41), most total bases (117), most runs batted in (39), and most homers hit by a catcher (12).

In all World Series history no catcher ever made more put-outs, more assists, more double plays, or handled more chances than the amazing Yogi. And no player ever derived as much money from World Series competition. Yogi netted record earnings of $78,225 in fall classics. No wonder he has come to be known as "Mr. World Series," for he may never be equaled as a record-breaker in the fall classic.

No one actually knows how Lawrence Peter Berra came by his curious nickname of Yogi. But history always will know how this once ugly-duckling and diamond clown came by his everlasting fame as baseball's greatest catcher. The fantastic rags-to-riches saga of Yogi Berra is an American success story to inspire all boys who believe in baseball miracles.

William Malcolm (Bill) Dickey

JUNE 6, 1907—

IN THE 16 years he was a big-league catcher, William Dickey played in the shadow of some of baseball's most fabulous and glamorous stars. Everyone took the quiet, hard-working backstop for granted. To all, he was just plain Bill. Yet there never was a more skillful, more durable, or more versatile catcher in the majors.

In his unobtrusive and modest way, Bill Dickey accomplished enough to merit election to baseball's Hall of Fame.

A native of Bastrop, Louisiana, Bill was only 18 when he began to play professional baseball. His father, a railroad conductor who had played local baseball, gave him encouragement. For several years Bill drifted around the minors learning the baseball trade. Finally, late in 1928, the New York Yankees bought him for $12,500.

When the Yankee manager first saw rookie Bill Dickey behind home plate, he told the unimpressed club owner:

"We've bought a player who is going to be one of the greatest catchers in the game."

Bill Dickey became more than that. He became baseball's perfect catcher. He played 16 seasons for the Yankees, and his deeds were more durable than dramatic. He rarely missed a game. He never complained, and never looked for an excuse to pass up a catching assignment. Fingers broken by foul tips, bruises, spike wounds — nothing ever kept Bill from playing. Once he was hospitalized as a result of a beaning. A short time later, hard-working Bill was back in the lineup, and in that campaign of 1941, he caught his 100th game for the 13th consecutive season — a major league record that still stands.

Bill set several astonishing catching records. One season he compiled a .996 fielding average. He played through 125 games without a passed ball. He batted-in 133 runs in one season. He wound up with a .313 lifetime batting average and 1,969 hits.

A smart, clear-thinking catcher, Bill Dickey handled pitchers superbly. His direction of the Yankee team was flawless. He seldom called a wrong pitch. He had incredible insight into the habits of every man who came to bat. Once he spotted a batter's weakness, he never forgot it. And his sign-stealing skill was amazing.

Ironically, though Bill was one of the most gentlemanly and inoffensive of players, he starred in one of the most memorable brawls ever staged on a big-league diamond. It marked the first and only time the quiet man lost his temper. On a steaming-hot July 4th afternoon in 1932, coming into home plate, Carl Reynolds of the Washington Senators crashed into catcher Dickey and bowled him over. Furious, Bill picked himself off the ground, and threw one punch at the player who had roughed him up. It broke his jaw. It also touched off one of the wildest free-for-all riots in major-league history.

For this irresponsible act, the great Yankee catcher was fined $1,000 and suspended for 30 days. It was the most severe penalty ever imposed on a big-league player for fighting. To the end of his distinguished career, Bill Dickey regretted that violent outburst of temper. He never again raised a hand in anger to another player, regardless of the provocation.

Bill Dickey was almost 40 when his playing days finally came to an end, much to the regret of the Yankees. In the 16 seasons he had been their catcher, he had helped them win nine pennants and eight World Series championships.

No longer a big-league catcher, Bill Dickey became a Yankee coach. He taught his successor to catch so well that that pupil, Yogi Berra, became the most famous catcher of all time.

In 1954, William Malcolm Dickey was named to the Hall of Fame.

Roy Campanella

NOVEMBER 19, 1921—

LOS ANGELES DODGERS

EVER SINCE he was a ragged little boy growing up on the slum streets of Philadelphia, Roy Campanella's one dream in life was to play baseball. No youngster ever played the game with more gusto or greater joy.

He was only 15 years old when he became a professional baseball player. A team of grown men had offered him $25 a week to be their catcher, for weekend games only. At first Roy's mother, a deeply religious woman, was against it.

"My son won't play baseball if he must work on Sundays," she said. "It's a day for churchgoing. My boy must have time to pray on Sundays."

It was agreed that Roy would play mostly on Saturdays, and on Sundays only after he had gone to church. For his first baseball trip away from home, Roy's mother gave him a Bible for guidance. It remained his traveling companion to the end of his baseball days.

At 16, Roy was a full-fledged pro ballplayer. He was a catcher for seven days a week, summer and winter. He barnstormed all over the United States and South America. He caught more than 300 games a year, and earned almost $300 a month. For 12 years he was a baseball gypsy.

Finally the color line in major league baseball was broken, and in 1948 Roy came to the big leagues to catch for the Brooklyn Dodgers. He was 27 years old.

When roly-poly Roy squatted behind home plate to catch his first major-league game, it was a memorable day for the national pastime. He was the first Negro catcher in big-league history.

Playing every game with the ecstasy of a man who loved his work, affable Roy became the happiest warrior of the majors. No player was ever more popular with his teammates than easygoing Roy. But even more, he was a great catcher. His quickness behind the plate was astonishing. He wasted no motion getting his throws to all bases. His rifle arm nipped a host of surprised base runners. Roy achieved a phenomenal record of throwing out would-be base stealers. In his first 600 major-league games, he nailed 150 base stealers out of 200. He became one of the greatest pick-off artists in history.

One of the brainiest of catchers, Roy also became the greatest backstop slugger in National League history. No big-league catcher ever hit as many home runs in a single season as Roy did in 1953 — he belted 41 of them. That season he set another all-time record by batting in 142 runs. He set another all-time record for catchers by collecting 807 putouts in one season. He hit more home runs than any other backstop in league history — 242.

Although he suffered numerous injuries — broken hands, chipped elbows, pulled muscles, strained ligaments, torn knees, spike wounds, and once even temporary blindness — Roy always caught more than 100 games each season.

In less than ten full seasons in the big leagues, Roy sparked the Dodgers to five pennants. No wonder he became the highest-paid catcher in National League history, as well as the only backstop to win the league's Most Valuable Player award three times.

Although Campy became one of baseball's greatest stars, he carried his fame with modesty and dignity. He became a baseball idol to boys all over America, yet he was never too busy to talk to his fans, nor to help, advise, and guide troubled youngsters.

The fabulous big-league career of baseball's happiest player came to a shocking and tragic end. In 1958 an automobile accident left Roy with a broken neck and partial paralysis — forced to spend the rest of his life in a wheelchair.

But in the greatest tragedy of his life Roy proved himself to be an even greater and more courageous champion than he had been in baseball. Although an invalid, he refused to remain helpless or useless. He became a baseball coach, a radio and television sports commentator, a lecturer, and an author, too. His heroic comeback inspired other unfortunates the world over.

Once Ray said, "You have to be a man to be a big leaguer, but you have to have a lot of little boy in you, too." He was both.

Although he played in the big leagues less than a decade, catcher Roy Campanella will be remembered as long as baseball is played.

Denton True (Cy) Young

MARCH 29, 1867—NOVEMBER 4, 1955

THE SPORTING NEWS

CY YOUNG was a gangling Ohio farm boy of 23 when, in the summer of 1890, the Cleveland baseball club hired him to pitch in the big leagues for $75 a month. The sight of the big hayseed going to the mound to pitch his first major-league game brought laughter from rival players and even his own teammates. The 200-pound, 6-foot-2 rube was dressed in a patched-up baseball uniform several sizes too small for him. But in his major-league debut, the ill-clad rookie hurled a brilliant three-hitter, and nobody ever again laughed at pitcher Young.

Nicknamed "Cyclone" because of his whirlwind speed, Cy Young became the most wondrous pitcher of all. A hurler with a rubber arm, the amazing right-hander accomplished incredible feats. No one pitched in the majors as long, or participated in as many games as Cy Young. He pitched in 906 contests over a period of 22 years.

For 16 years he won 20 or more games a season. Five times he won more than 30 games a season. While scoring his many victories, he struck out 2,819 batters.

79

He was the first in history to pitch three no-hit, no-run games. Only Cy Young ever hurled no-hitters in both major leagues. He was the first in the 20th century to pitch a perfect no-hit game. Once he pitched 23 consecutive innings without allowing a hit. Another time he hurled a walkless, 20-inning victory. When he was 40 years old he was still so astounding a mound marvel that he pitched 35 complete games for a tail-end team, and won 22 of them. Fantastic pitcher that he was, the "Old Master" was no weakling at bat. He made 638 hits, more hits during his career than any other pitcher in history. Also, he scored 328 runs, more runs than any other pitcher.

Although Cy Young never was paid more than $5,000 a season, the winningest pitcher of all time was a player beyond reproach, and the soul of honesty. Once gamblers offered him a bribe of $20,000 to "throw" just one game. Angrily, he threw the men out of his hotel room, then went to the ball park and pitched one of his finest winning games.

On a blistering hot afternoon in 1911, when he was past 44, Cy Young lost a gruelling 1-to-0 hurling duel to a sensational rookie half his age, Grover Cleveland Alexander. It was Cy Young's last game in the majors.

"It's time to quit when the kids begin to beat you," he said sadly. Although his rubber arm was as good as ever, he decided to call it a career, not because he had grown too old, but because he had grown too fat to field bunts.

When he left the big leagues Cy Young was an awesome legend. He had left behind him the all-time winning record of 511 major-league victories! That mark will probably stand for all time.

Denton True Young is still an inspiration to big-league hurlers. Today, at the end of every season, the Cy Young Memorial Award is given to the outstanding major-league pitcher of the year. This "Oscar" from the "Old Master" is the highest honor a pitcher can win.

Walter Perry Johnson

NOVEMBER 6, 1887–
DECEMBER 10, 1946

AS A BOY growing up on an isolated farm in Humboldt, Kansas, Walter Johnson had little chance to play baseball. He was almost 20 when a traveling salesman saw him pitch in a sandlot game. The excited drummer dispatched urgent letters to all the major-league clubs, extolling the virtues of the unknown sandlot pitcher. But all ignored the raves from that self-appointed baseball scout. Eventually the Washington Senators expressed some interest, and picked up pitcher Walter Johnson for the price of a $9 railroad ticket.

On August 2, 1907, Walter Johnson pitched his first major-league game. He lost it. But with that initial defeat, began the fabulous saga of "The Big Train" — the hurler who threw a ball faster than anybody who ever lived!

There was no mystery to the pitching magic of right-hander Johnson. He had two pitches: fast and faster. With each pitch he poured forth lightning. For 21 years he pitched for the lowly Washington Senators, a perennial second-division club. During that time he created records almost beyond belief.

When Walter Johnson was still a green rookie, he performed an incredible feat that set the pattern for his future greatness. In a tough three-game series against the Yankees, he pitched all three games in only four days, allowed only 12 hits, and won each game by a shutout. It was the most fabulous trio of triumphs ever won by a freshman pitcher.

As the years went by, The Big Train became history's greatest opening-day pitcher. He invariably hurled the inaugural game for the Senators. His record-making total was 14 opening-day games. He won nine of these inaugural contests, seven of them by shutouts — also a record.

He was the only pitcher in history to hurl 5,924 innings. Only Johnson ever pitched 531 complete major-league games, ever pitched 113 shutouts, ever hurled 56 consecutive scoreless innings. In 1912 he won 16 games in a row. It still stands as an American League record. He set other records — for most games started, most chances accepted by a pitcher, and the best fielding by a big-league hurler. Twelve times he won 20 or more games a season. Twice he won more than 30 games a campaign.

No pitcher ever struck out as many batters as speedballer Johnson. He whiffed 3,508 men! The record is likely to stand for all time.

The greater the odds against him, the more remarkable was his pitching. Only once did he complain of having a sore arm. Nevertheless, that day he went to the mound to pitch, for he was unwilling to disappoint the huge crowd jamming the ball park. Suffering pain with every throw, Johnson pitched the full game. As if as a reward, he wound up that painful afternoon by pitching the only no-hit, no-run game of his fabulous career.

Walter Johnson was more than just an incredible hurler

who won 416 major-league games. He was the most beloved pitcher baseball ever had. He was a diamond idol for a whole nation — from the President of the United States to the youngest schoolboy. No baseball hero was ever more modest, more sportsmanlike, or a finer gentleman. He never smoked, drank, or swore. He never feuded with players, or argued with umpires.

Fantastic pitcher that he was, he had to wait 17 frustrating years before his team finally won a pennant, so he could pitch in a World Series. He beat the Giants in a 12-inning thriller, the seventh and deciding game of the 1924 classic. It gave Washington its first world's championship. That heroic victory created such a wave of wild and joyous sentiment that grown men cried and there was dancing in the streets.

He became a legend during his lifetime, and he still remains a legend in Washington. The memory of The Big Train is kept alive, year after year, at ceremonies in which many notables, baseball fans, and thousands of kids participate. A wreath is laid at his monument, which stands at the entrance to the Washington ball park. There is a Walter Johnson baseball league, a street is named after this Hall of Fame pitcher, and in Bethesda, Maryland, a suburb of Washington, there is now a Walter Johnson High School. It's the only school in the world named after a baseball hero.

Christopher (Big Six) Mathewson

AUGUST 12, 1880–OCTOBER 7, 1925

CHRISTY MATHEWSON was born with a genteel, if not a silver, spoon in his mouth. His father was a gentleman farmer in a small town in Pennsylvania. His parents' dream was for their son to become a minister when he grew up.

At Bucknell University the handsome 6-footer was an honor student, president of his class, and a member of the glee club and literary societies. He was also a star football and basketball player, and the best pitcher the college ever had.

He was barely 20 when, in 1900, he became a major-league pitcher for the former New York Giants. He was a strange kind of ballplayer for that rough-and-tumble baseball era. Soft-spoken, well-mannered, always the perfect gentleman, Matty was one of the first college-bred athletes to play in the big leagues. He remained with the Giants for 17 years and became America's first great sports idol!

A nation of youngsters worshipped him as a diamond superman. He was everybody's ideal of pitching perfection. He pitched with such grace and ease that even rival hurlers found it a pleasure to watch him. A self-taught pitcher, right-hander Mathewson developed his own stuff — and he had stuff no other big-league hurler ever had. His most famous pitch was the fadeaway.

There never lived a pitcher with greater control than Matty the Great. In 1908, while winning 37 games, he pitched 391 innings, but walked only 42 batters! In 1913 he pitched 306 innings, faced 1,195 batters, but yielded only 21 bases on balls. That season, while pitching his team to a pennant with

25 victories, Matty set a fantastic record for control pitching which is likely to stand for all time. He hurled 68 consecutive innings without issuing one walk!

Four times he won 30 or more games a season; 13 times he won 20 or more games a season. He pitched the Giants to five pennants. In 1905, Matty performed the greatest hurling feat in all World Series history. Within a period of only five days he pitched three complete games — and won all by shutouts!

In the 17 seasons he starred in the majors, he pitched two no-hitters, struck out 2,505 men, and won 373 games. No pitcher in the history of the National League ever won more contests.

Few heroes in baseball history ever commanded the love, respect, and adoration that Christopher Mathewson enjoyed all his life. A religious man, he never once pitched on Sunday. Clergymen hailed him as a model for all to follow. His teammates idolized him for his thoughtful acts, unselfishness, modesty, and sense of honor. He was so honest that even the umpires used to take his word on doubtful decisions. He was more than a baseball idol. He was an ideal.

An inspiration to the national pastime, Christy Mathewson was so popular a baseball hero that in 1918, at a Liberty Bond drive, a baseball bearing his autograph was auctioned off for more than a million dollars!

In 1936 he was elected to the Hall of Fame.

Grover Cleveland (Pete) Alexander

FEBRUARY 26, 1887—NOVEMBER 4, 1950

HE WAS a gangling, freckle-faced, sandy-haired farm boy from Nebraska when he came into professional baseball at the age of 20. In 1911 the Philadelphia Phillies needed an extra pitcher and reluctantly bought him from a minor-league club for a paltry $750. His starting salary in the majors was just $900 a season. But from the very beginning Grover Cleveland Alexander was a star. In his first major-league year he won 28 games for the Phillies. No other rookie hurler in modern baseball history ever matched that record!

Pitching with effortless grace and uncanny control, right-hander Alexander established himself as the smoothest hurler there ever was. He created mound masterpieces and set major-league records that still stand.

He pitched in more games than any other hurler in National League history (696). He won 373, matching Christy Mathewson's record.

Once he hurled a full nine-inning game in the record time of only 58 minutes. Twice he pitched and won both ends of a double-header. Four times in the 1915 season he hurled one-hit games. It is an all-time record for one season. In 1916 he pitched 16 shutouts. This is also an all-time record for a single season. Alex pitched a total of 90 shutouts, for a lifetime National League record. In three consecutive seasons he won 30 or more games!

In 1918, at the height of his fame as a mound marvel, he deserted the majors to shoulder a rifle and fight for his country in World War I. Sergeant Alexander saw bloody action on the battlefields of Europe before he came home to pitch again in the big leagues. Although he had lost some of the zip from his fast ball, was sick from exposure to poison gas, and had become subject to sudden epileptic seizures, he was still a pitcher of matchless effectiveness. In 1920 he won 27 games for the Chicago Cubs. When he was past 40, his sidearm curves and amazing control won 21 games for the St. Louis Cardinals.

During his fabulous big-league career, Alexander struck out 2,227 batters. Ironically, he is best remembered for just one strikeout which he achieved when he was an old pitcher, supposedly on his last legs.

It happened in the seventh and final game of the 1926 World Series between the St. Louis Cardinals and the New York Yankees. In the seventh inning of that deciding game, with two outs, the bases full, and the feared Yankee slugger Tony Lazzeri at bat, old Alex was called from the bullpen to rescue his team from disaster. Only the previous day he had pitched and won his second game of that World Series. Now the weary veteran was expected to stop the fierce Yankee rally and protect a slim one-run lead. He struck out Tony Lazzeri on four pitches. He silenced the mighty Yankee bats for the rest of that game to win for the St. Louis Cardinals their first World Series championship. The drama of that historic strikeout became a diamond epic.

Old Pete Alexander was past 43 when he pitched his last game in the major leagues. Twenty seasons he had been there. In 1938, elected to the Hall of Fame, he was a man who became a legend in his own lifetime.

But Old Alex was his own worst enemy. In the twilight years of his life his drinking caught up with him. He died penniless and friendless. It was a pathetic finish for the pitching wonder who once had been honored and cheered as Alexander the Great!

Robert William Andrew (Bob) Feller

NOVEMBER 3, 1918—

WHEN BOB FELLER was born on a farm in Van Meter, Iowa, his father dedicated him to baseball. Farmer Bill Feller, who once had been a semi-pro baseball player, told his friends:

"I don't want my son to be a farmer. Robert will be a baseball player, and do what I never could. Someday he'll be good enough to play in the big leagues!"

Bobby was six years old when his father began to teach him how to pitch a baseball. As the boy grew older, he and his dad held daily practice sessions in the cow pasture behind the barn. He learned to hurl a ball with such speed that once a fast pitch broke three of his father's ribs. But the daily baseball lessons did not stop.

Before he was 14 Bobby was good enough to pitch for a local baseball team of grown men. He was still in high school, only 17 years old, when the Cleveland Indians snared him to pitch in the big leagues. On August 23, 1936, Bobby Feller pitched his first game in the majors. It was the most auspicious and sensational debut in big-league history! Pitching against the former St. Louis Browns, the "boy wonder" struck out eight of the first nine men to face him. He won his first game with an impressive total of 15 strikeouts. It was the greatest pitching "first" ever recorded! Only three weeks later, in another game, fireballer Feller fanned 17 batters.

As the seasons went by, Bobby Feller enriched his fame as a true strike-out king. Fifty times he fanned ten or more batters in a game. In 1938 he became the first modern pitcher in history to strike out 18 men in a single nine-inning game.

90

WIDE WORLD

In only four seasons, while winning 93 games, Rapid Robert hurled 1,238 innings, and struck out 1,007 men!

The kid with the bashful grin and the blinding fast ball achieved fantastic pitching feats. In 1940 he became the first and only hurler in history to pitch a no-hit, no-run game on the opening day of a new baseball season. Also, he became the only pitcher of the 20th century to hurl three no-hitters! His incredible total of 12 one-hit games stands today as a record.

In 1941, when Bobby was at the height of his fame as the phenomenal "boy wonder" of the majors, he heard his country's call and enlisted in the United States Navy to fight in World War II. Nearly four years were to pass before he returned to pitch in the majors again. Though Bob Feller had been away from baseball 44 months, he achieved his greatest strikeout feat upon his return. In 1946 he pitched 371 innings, won 26 games, and struck out 348 men. It's the all-time record for strikeouts in a single season.

A stickler for clean living, Bobby Feller became not only the highest-paid pitcher in baseball of his time, but also an inspiring model for the youth of America. He was 37 when he closed his fabulous career in the big leagues. Although a war had robbed him of nearly four of his best young years as a big-league pitcher, he still left the majors with an awesome record of 266 victories and 2,581 strikeouts.

He was always grateful to the man who had introduced him to baseball in his infancy. In 1962 Bob Feller finally achieved the highest honor that can be bestowed upon a great player. He was elected to baseball's Hall of Fame. When he was asked who had inspired and helped him most to achieve his immortality as a big-league pitcher, simply but proudly he answered, "My father!"

Warren Spahn

APRIL 23, 1921—

BORN in Buffalo, New York, the son of a wallpaper salesman, Warren Spahn began pitching a baseball before he had
learned the alphabet. His first diamond was the backyard of
the Spahn home, and his first baseball teacher was his father,
a frustrated semi-pro third baseman. While still a boy in
elementary school, young Warren never missed a daily baseball practice session with his dedicated father, who strove to
mold him into a ballplayer.

At 13 Warren was playing baseball with a team of grown
men. His father played third base for the same team and the
Spahn father-and-son combination was a local sensation.

When he finished high school Warren became a pitcher in
professional baseball for $80 a month. His pro career began
and almost finished at the same time. He tore tendons in his
left shoulder, and had to quit pitching in mid-season. The
following year when he resumed his career, a thrown ball
broke his nose and disfigured him for life.

Despite tough breaks, Warren was not discouraged. He
was determined to justify his father's confidence in him, and
become a big-league player. In 1942, when he was 20, he
came to the big leagues to pitch for the Boston Braves, now
of Milwaukee. But before Warren could win even one game
in the majors, he left the big leagues to fight in World War II.

For the next three years Sergeant Spahn had no hope of
ever again pitching in the big leagues. He even despaired
of returning home alive. But he did come back, bringing with
him battlefield decorations, a Presidential citation for brav-
ery, and a set of jittery nerves.

WIDE WORLD

When the war-shaken southpaw returned to the big leagues to pitch again he was most unimpressive. In his first full season in the majors Warren barely managed to win eight games. But in the next season he won 21 games and was on the way to his baseball destiny.

As the years passed this modest and gentlemanly left hander grew in greatness as a pitcher. Even in defeat he achieved marvelous feats. Once, while losing two consecutive heartbreaking pitching duels, he set a major-league record by striking out 29 men.

Southpaw Spahn became one of the greatest strikeout artists in history. For 16 straight seasons he fanned more than 100 batters a campaign. Also, he became the only left-hander in history to win 20 or more games a season 12 times. He became the highest-paid pitcher in the history of the National League.

In 1961, although Warren Spahn was the oldest pitcher in the National League (past 40), he had one of the finest seasons of his long and fabulous career. He won 21 games in 1961. He also hurled the only no-hitter in the majors that year. He led his league in earned runs and led both leagues in completed games, with 21. He stretched his record of "most shutouts by a left-hander" to 55. And he extended his lifetime victory total to 309 major-league triumphs, making him the winningest left-handed pitcher in baseball history.

ABOUT THE AUTHOR

MAC DAVIS is a born storyteller, as readers of his many popular sports books know. For years his prolific typewriter has pounded out amazing, colorful, and never-before-told sports yarns for books, magazines, and newspapers.

His unusual stories have been broadcast by the best-known sports commentators, on hundreds of radio stations all over the world. Davis' dramatic sports shows have been heard and seen on radio and television by millions of people.

The Greatest in Baseball gives sports fans of all ages an exciting and intimate glimpse into the wonderful world of baseball, revealing the human side of baseball's greatest heroes.

Other Sports Books by Mac Davis:

100 Greatest Sports Heroes
Teen-age Baseball Jokes and Legends
Great American Sports Humor
Sports Shorts
Say It Ain't So